GRACE KELLY

A life in pictures Edited by Yann-Brice Dherbier & Pierre-Henri Verlhac

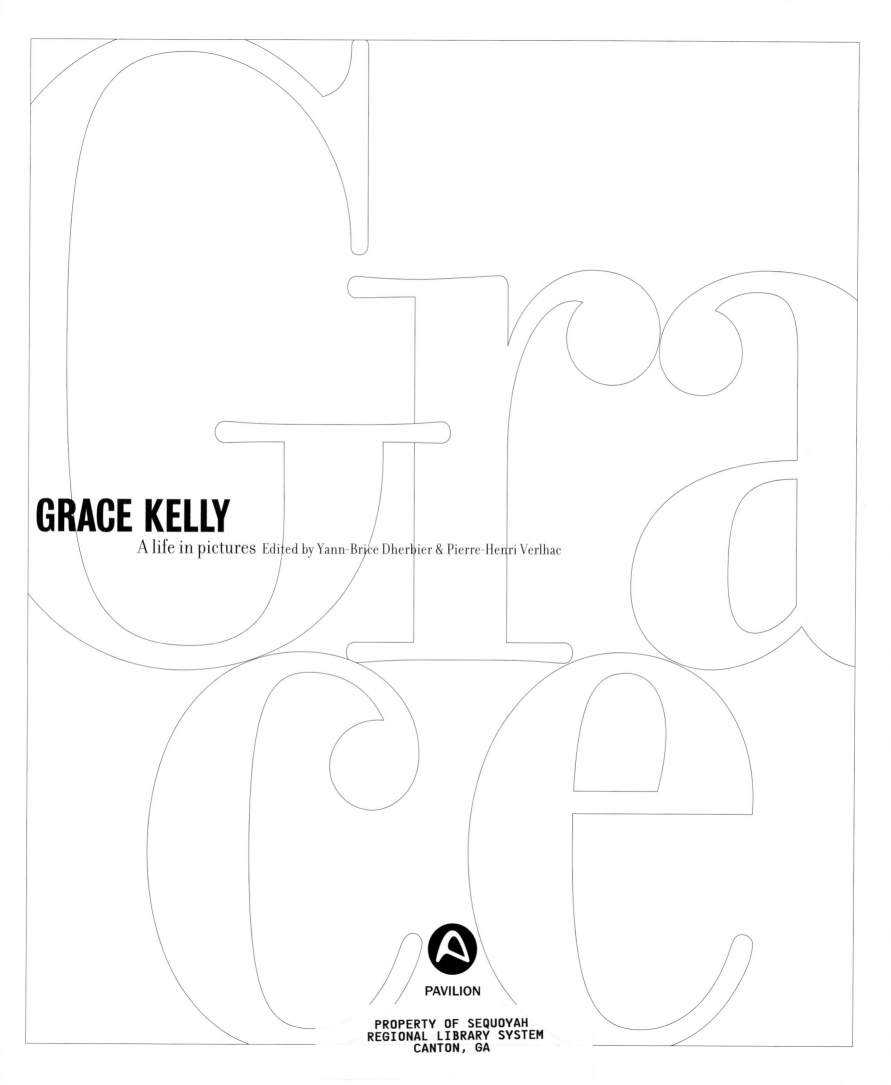

PAVILION

My mother was photographed countless times, by the world's best photographers. However, what was most entrancing about her was her compassion and generosity of spirit. She didn't pose in order to become beautiful. She simply was beautiful. The photographs in this book – unseen until now – help show why.

His Serene Highness Prince Albert II, June 2006

Foreword

Grace Kelly was the fairest of them all. As a fashion designer, I constantly consider the power of pop culture and the style icons of our time. Why are we fascinated by some stars, while we are indifferent to others? Why do we pay to see them, or wish to be like them? With Grace Kelly, answers to these questions are more complicated than they at first might appear.

People often talk about Grace Kelly as 'porcelain perfection'. As far as I am concerned, this label completely misses the point. I never met Grace Kelly, but somehow I feel as if I knew her. She strikes me as having been very well grounded – a real person who found herself in some highly unusual situations. She was a world-famous movie star, but for most of her life she chose to be a loyal wife, a dedicated mother, and a faithful friend. Involved with countless charities, she was truly a humanitarian. What might be a cliché under different circumstances in her case was literally true. She had an inner beauty that shone.

Her looks were simple, clean and classic. She was a natural beauty, not at all pretentious or overdone. Grace Kelly didn't have to worry about hair and make-up, or being weighed down with jewellery. She was refreshingly wholesome, confident, compassionate and full of poise. Purity, I believe, was her greatest asset.

She made a great impact in a small amount of time. It's surprising to remember how few movies she actually made. The one that really gives me the chills is *To Catch a Thief*. The movie was set on the French Riviera, which is one of my favourite places in the world. Add Grace Kelly to that spectacular setting, and the Côte d'Azur's ambience really blossoms.

By this point in her career, she'd been included on numerous best-dressed lists and was heralded internationally as a paragon of style. She made it look impossibly easy. Grace Kelly didn't follow fashion trends, but made her own. For example, unlike any other actresses then or since, she always wore white gloves around Los Angeles – she exuded glamour by simply being herself. She became an icon without trying.

She was vital. She glowed. Back in the 1950s, the word 'marvellous' was popular and quite overused. But, for Grace Kelly, it was absolutely accurate. You didn't look at her up there on screen. You marvelled.

At the age of 26, she quit acting. She was a top box-office draw, an Academy Award winner, and yet she walked away from it all. She went out with a bang in her last film, *High Society*. In it, she sings her first song on screen, Cole Porter's *True Love*, a duet with co-star Bing Crosby. I suspect she sang extremely well because she'd found her own true love: Prince Rainier III of Monaco. She went from reel royalty to real royalty.

Being Her Serene Highness was a much more demanding role than any she'd ever had before. She went from living under the spotlight to dwelling under a microscope. But it didn't seem to bother her one bit. Not only did she quickly adjust, she triumphed.

It's an incredible, inspirational life, and now we are fortunate to have these glimpses of her, as never seen before until this book.

As I turn these pages, I'm mindful there will never be another Grace Kelly. Other natural beauties may emerge in the spotlight, but she was one of a kind.

Tommy Hilfiger, June 2006

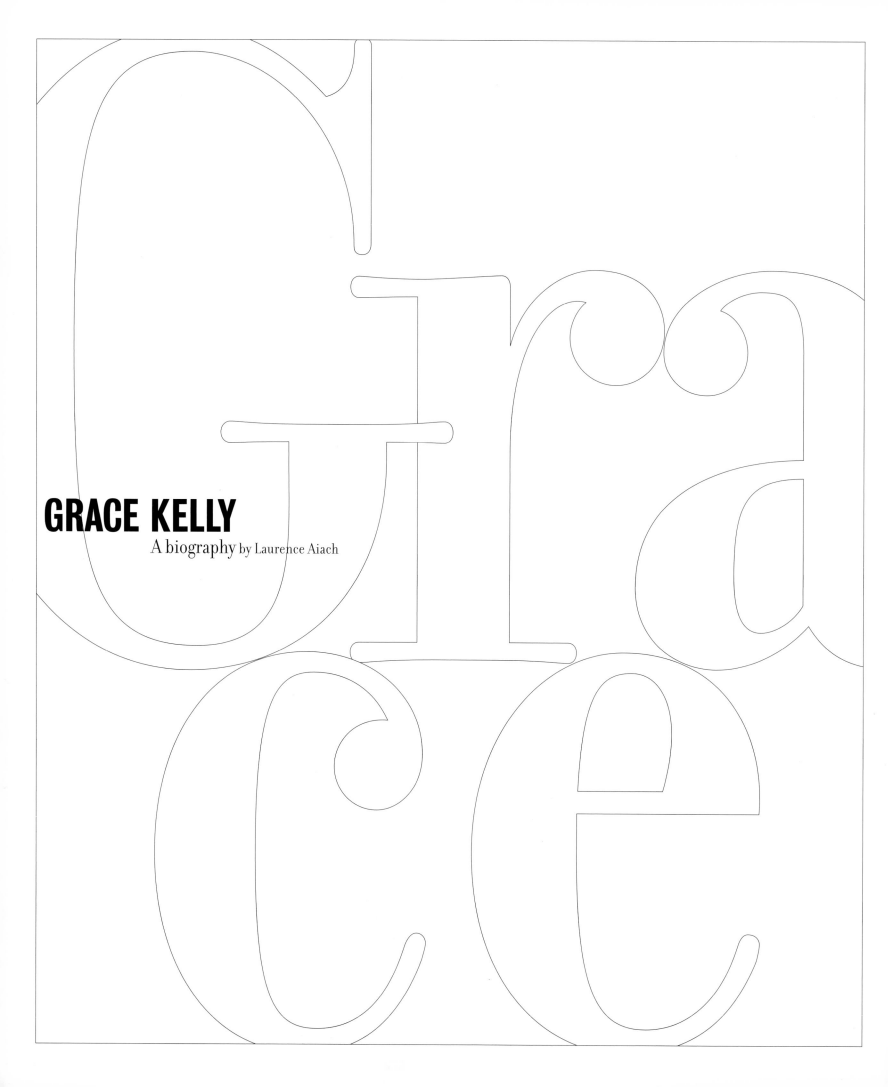

GRACE KELLY

A biography by Laurence Aiach

GRACE KELLY

There once was a princess with the sweet name of Grace... Just as in all the fairy tales, her story could have started this way. But Grace Kelly was much more than this. A talented comedienne, an exquisite beauty, a young woman from a wealthy family who became royalty – Grace Kelly lived many lives.

The Kellys were of Irish origin and fiercely proud of their heritage, which they demonstrated at any given opportunity. Grace's grandfather, John Henry, fleeing the famine and the bloody insurrections of the second half of the 19th century, set sail for the New World at the age of 20. He settled in Schuylkill (now Philadephia), on the east coast of the United States, and started a family with a young Irish woman who, like him, came from County Mayo.

They were to have 10 children, among them the father of Grace, John Brendan. Too poor to send all their children to school, the Kellys sent the first seven to work in a factory while the rest went to school. John Brendan was one of the lucky three. He grew up to be a young man toughened by sport, and the Christian values instilled in him made him a man of irreproachable morals. He joined the army and left for France during World War I. As a gifted boxer, he earned the title of champion of the American infantry.

On his return he joined his brother's construction business as a bricklayer. Then, slowly, he started building up his own business. Thanks to a loan of $7000 he set up his own construction company, Kelly for Brickwork, which grew into an empire. Decades later, at the time of his daughter's marriage, his fortune was valued at 18 million dollars.

A brilliant entrepreneur, a popular and respected man, John B Kelly was also an accomplished athlete. He was passionate about rowing and won a gold medal at the Olympic Games at Antwerp in 1920, for sculling. In 1924 he married a beautiful young woman of German origin, Margaret Majer. Also a decorated athlete, she would become an instructor in physical education and the first female athletics coach for coeds, at the University of Pennsylvania. The young newlyweds set up their home in a comfortable suburb of Philadelphia, East Falls. They had four children: Margaret (called Peggy), John Jr, Grace Patricia and Elizabeth-Anne (called Lizanne).

The model little girl

Brought up in a lovely 17-roomed house, the Kelly children were deprived of nothing. A black servant, Godfrey Ford, looked after them day and night. In this huge home overlooking a landscaped garden, little Grace, born on November 12, 1929, would grow up leading a sheltered life. However, as an asthmatic, she spent a good part of her childhood bedridden. Often afflicted by colds or chest pains, she was by far the most fragile child in the family. While her brother and sisters played outside, she spent entire days in her bedroom. The dolls she played with were her only friends. Calm, docile, timid, shortsighted, awkward, introverted and dreamy, Grace displayed from her earliest years a 'tranquillity of the soul', as her mother would say.

Even when accosted by her sisters, she never fought with them. She didn't rebel against anything, not even her bad health. Isolated by her fragile condition, Grace created her own world, peopled with dolls and fantasy heroes to whom she told her stories all alone in her room, in the garden or in the cupboard where she often hid. 'Goldilocks', as her parents called her, was definitely a child apart. Unlike them, she wasn't at all sporty and showed no desire for competition.

Her mother, a strong character, was authority personified. Nicknamed 'The Chief' or 'The Prussian General' by her children, 'Ma' Kelly maintained an almost military atmosphere in the household. Her displays of affection were rare. She did not exactly cover her children with kisses – far from it. In the Kelly home, time was king and no one, not even the head of the family, dared be late for anything. Economical, organised, orderly, severe, Grace's mother planned the days of the household down to the last minute.

As good Catholics, they went to Mass every Sunday and every meal was preceded with a grace. Between the ages of six and 14, little Grace Patricia attended Ravenhill Academy, in the good care of the Assumption Sisters. An icon of intelligence and daintiness, she was a model little girl. She was a good pupil, studious and disciplined, and participated in numerous works of charity. Her strict upbringing taught her never to feel sorry for herself. The little girl adored animals, and dogs in particular. She was also fascinated by the princesses Elizabeth and Margaret of England. Insatiable, she collected every snippet of information she could find about them and every article relating to their royal lives.

By far the least athletic member of the family, Grace showed an interest in the arts from a young age. She was gifted in music, drawing and writing, and at the age of eight wanted to become a ballerina. In the course of her dance classes she took her first steps in children's theatre. From the age of six, she performed with her brother and sisters and staged spectacles for the neighbourhood, playing the part of the Virgin Mary or Cinderella. At 12 she made her stage début at East Falls in the play *Don't Feed the Animals*. Aware of the talent already evident in their daughter, the Kellys were persuaded that their child had a gift for the stage.

Tall and slim, with delicate features, her face still childlike, timid and prone to blushing, young Grace became a young woman. She increasingly drew the attention of the opposite sex, but she was embarrassed by their compliments and her attraction to the male of the species was never more than a passing fancy. Having just turned 14, she entered Stevens School in Germantown. There, too, her beautiful manners, her wit and her poise distinguished her easily among the other young women.

By 16, Grace Kelly was 1.67 metres tall, a keen swimmer and loved watching musical comedies at the cinema. She was tempted to study the dramatic arts, but she was not accepted at the prestigious Bennington College in Vermont. When she and her parents toured Europe during the summer of 1947, Grace took advantage of the trip to visit London and its theatres. On her return her mind was made up: she would become a comedienne.

New York

At seventeen, she left the family cocoon and Philadelphia for New York. Her aim was to be accepted at the American Academy of Dramatic Arts there. At her audition for a place at the Academy, the professors judged her to have real potential, even if her voice was 'nasal' and 'improperly placed'. She was accepted at the Academy in October 1947.

Like many other young women from good families, she stayed at the Barbizon Hotel for Women, an 'establishment for single ladies' in New York. For almost two years she learned dancing, diction and theatrical expression. A dedicated and conscientious student, she spent her days and nights studying. For her, it mattered only that she did not disappoint her parents. Since it was out of the question to ask her father for financial assistance, she became a model to earn some money. Very quickly, the photo sessions built up. As a model she advertised cigarettes, then soap, and went on to cosmetics and hairstyles, and soon had a comfortable life free of need. Gradually, her modelling extended from magazine covers to television where her natural ease in front of the camera became evident.

In her second year at the Academy of Dramatic Arts, her professor was a certain Don Richardson. Tall, dark and handsome, and of a mature age, he melted the beauty's heart. He became her first love. When she took him home to present him to her parents, the dinner turned into a fiasco. Soon afterwards, the relationship came to an end.

Once she graduated, Grace Kelly set off on the route followed by all first-time actors. From auditions to hopeful interviews, she did the rounds of the agencies to try to get a role. During this time she became aware of an annoying handicap: she was too tall for her male partners!

Grace criss-crossed America to play on provincial stages. In 1949, at the age of 20, she landed her first Broadway role in the play *The Father*, by August Strindberg. With barely any experience to speak of, and sick with nerves, she went on stage on opening night to face the public and her entire family. In spite of the moderate success of the play it closed after two months, but the actress in Grace Kelly was well and truly born.

Edith Van Cleve became her agent in 1950. Like all actresses worthy of the name, Grace Kelly went to live in Manhattan. Quickly, she was attracted to the world of television. Between the adaptation of a novel by F. Scott Fitzgerald (*Rich Boy*), a series (*Berkeley Square*) and a role as a music-hall singer in *Lights Out* she performed in *The Way of the Eagle* with the French comedian Jean-Pierre Aumont. To begin with, Grace was distant, reserved and very polite towards her partner. Her 'Mister Aumont' irritated him enormously! But gradually, they became friends. Their love scenes for the film caused memorable moments of riotous laughter.

Constantly searching for an important cinema role, Grace Kelly never gave up. Television studios gave her work and for them at least her height did not pose a problem. But when she performed a screen test with the filmmaker Gregory Ratoff for *Taxi*, he was not convinced. However, her star was on the rise. John Ford and Alfred Hitchcock had both viewed the screen test. A little while later, Henri Hathaway gave her a small role in *Fourteen Hours*. It was her first film.

Her agent then suggested she perform in a less mainstream project. With no Indians and hardly a cowboy, with neither horse chases nor gunfire (or barely), the western *High Noon* was to irritate Hollywood. Not much impressed with the script, she hesitated, because she was being offered several plays at the time of the shooting. At the same time, United Artists were offering her a contract for three years... Could she refuse? Grace Kelly did not want to sell herself to Hollywood. Refusing to be a prisoner of a contract, she would not give up her freedom at any price. She held to her position and stitched up the shooting schedule and the studio. The making of the film was put off until autumn 1951 – and United Artists accepted a single contract for one film. Grace Kelly's star was in the ascendancy.

A star is born

Alone without her family, left to her own devices, isolated and lost, she did not cope well with her new life in Hollywood, nor with the pressure from the studios. Her lead man, Gary Cooper, was just as timid and reserved as herself, and she found little support anywhere. Worried by her state of mind, her mother sent her two sisters, Margaret and Lizanne, to be by Grace's side. All three of them moved to a suite in the prestigious Château Marmont, and the Kelly girls together enjoyed this life of splendour to the full.

They returned to New York once the shooting had finished, where Grace met an Irish comedian with whom she had her first real love affair. Of modest origins, in the throes of divorce and partial to alcohol, Gene Lyons was not warmly welcomed by the Kelly clan. Once again, family pressure won over her burgeoning romance and the relationship ended.

When *High Noon* premiered in 1952, the public was disconcerted by this atypical western and did not turn out in large numbers. But word of mouth spread the news and against all expectations the film was a triumph.

Gary Cooper carried off the Oscar for Best Actor for his performance. During this time, Grace was in her element in New York. She benefited from her anonymity, which allowed her to walk through the streets unrecognised. She went to galleries and museums. Far from the tumult of Hollywood and its stifling atmosphere, she came alive again.

The prestigious studio Metro Goldwyn Mayer, in search of new faces, offered her a contract for several years. She refused. But then she was offered a film shoot in Africa, for *Mogambo*. How could she not be excited by the prospect of performing in a film by John Ford, playing opposite Clark Gable and exploring Africa? Pressed by MGM, who worked hard to persuade her, Grace finally signed a contract for seven years with the studio... at the airport, just before flying to Kenya.

Despite the princely living conditions the actors enjoyed (Clark Gable, Ava Gardner and Grace), the shoot was a deluge of catastrophes. With everything from extreme heat, to the death of a member of the technical team, to tropical downpours, the socio-political climate and daily arguments between Ava Gardner and her husband (Frank Sinatra), the shoot was almost stopped several times. Nevertheless, Grace's vitality and love of life cheered everyone and contributed to bringing the actors together.

On returning to the United States, Grace was still under contract to MGM and she moved her bags indefinitely to Hollywood. When the film came out, *Mogambo* was a success. Grace was even nominated for an Oscar and won a Golden Globe award for Best Supporting Actress. But she was not quite a star and would have to wait before receiving the much coveted statuette.

Seeing her protégée down in the dumps now that she was once more far from her nearest and dearest, Grace's agent found her a role in a play performing in Philadelphia, *The Moon is Blue*. Grace had just arrived there when she learned that Warner wanted her for the next film from that master of suspense, Alfred Hitchcock.

Even though he had never seen her on the screen or the stage, but only in a screen test, Hitchcock was prepared to offer her the main female role. And so it was that, at the end of July 1953, Grace Kelly started her first film with the man who would become her teacher and Pygmalion. In *Dial M for Murder*, she was Margot. Under his direction for the first time, she became Hitchcock's 'It Girl'. Grace was 23 years old, and like a sculptor, Hitchcock shaped the young woman and created an ice-blonde femme fatale both inaccessible and fearless.

Several months after the film wrapped up, Grace was offered two interesting proposals: to play the partner of Marlon Brando in Elia Kazan's *On the Waterfront*, and to play at the side of James Stewart in Alfred Hitchcock's *Rear Window*. Preferring Hitchcock to Kazan, and Stewart to Marlon Brando, she gave up her role in Kazan's film to Eva Marie Saint.

The film crew, installed in a Paramount studio, soon discovered the marvels the master of suspense could produce. Grace Kelly, docilely following every step the director suggested to her, played the role that would make her a star, and she knew it. Amused by the image of an Ice Queen, she was in reality as mischievous and joyful as a child, but always undeniably focused and professional. 'Do you know that Grace Kelly, apparently so cold, hides a volcano of sensitivity, eroticism and passion?' asked Hitchcock. When the film came out in the summer of 1954, *Rear Window* was a huge success. The shoot had barely finished when she was involved in another film and then another... The two years, 1953 and 1954, were the most dynamic of her career. Over 13 months, Grace Kelly performed in six films (*Dial M for Murder*, *Rear Window*, *The Bridges at Toko-Ri*, *The Country Girl*, *Green Fire* and *To Catch a Thief*). The press fought for interviews and photo opportunities with the new darling of Hollywood.

A woman in love

In *The Bridges at Toko-Ri*, Grace played the part of the wife of William Holden. She succumbed to the charms of the actor, who was 12 years her senior and ... married! The friendship rapidly turned into a fiery passion. Besotted with Grace, Holden intended to divorce in order to marry her. Grace enthusiastically took Holden to Philadelphia to meet her family. Once again, the Kelly clan intervened. Assisted by Mrs Holden, they put an end to the liaison and the pair's plans. But several months later, a new film would reunite them. In *The Country Girl* Grace had as her partners William Holden and Bing Crosby. The trio's friendship was a romantic one. The two men, literally charmed by the young woman, were both her chivalrous servants. William Holden and Grace rediscovered each other and their passion. Bing Crosby would also engage in a fervent courtship with Grace, without success. When the shoot was finished, she took off to Colombia to play opposite Stuart Granger in *Green Fire*. During this time, Grace couldn't stop thinking about her next film.

Grace was impatient to rejoin Alfred Hitchcock, who was waiting for her on the Côte d'Azur to star in *To Catch a Thief*. She flew to Cannes in June 1954. There, she was happy. At the side of Cary Grant, she had great fun. Grant was a friend of Jackie Kennedy (later the wife of Aristotle Onassis) and took Grace with him for lunch on the yacht *Christina*, where she met the Greek millionaire.

During the film shoot, Grace was accompanied by Oleg Cassini, the well-known costume and fashion designer and a count of Italo-Russian origin who was close to the Kennedys. He would wait for months before the young woman gave in to his advances. After two divorces (one from Gene Tierney, mother of his two daughters) Cassini was once more a bachelor but didn't intend staying that way. He and Grace frequented the best restaurants of the Côte, and with her he was the most romantic of men. Under the Mediterranean sun, in an enchanting setting and far from Hollywood, Grace agreed to become his wife. However, alerted by the rumours and the photos that appeared in the press, Mr and Mrs Kelly formally opposed their union. In their eyes, Oleg Cassini was no more than a playboy. Grace renounced her planned marriage.

Physically exhausted and emotionally weary, the young woman returned to Los Angeles sadder than ever. The pitiless Californian world that she had never liked now seemed to her like hell. The 'gentle Miss Kelly' became capricious, irritable and volatile. Fits of tears, a loss of appetite – this crisis was the worst anyone who knew her had seen. In California she was isolated and everything around her seemed strange. Her life, her friends, her family and the film world disgusted her. She was even thinking of giving up her career. A crushing machine where only the box office mattered, Hollywood was the source of all she detested. She didn't want to live there any more or be subjected to the affronts of the headlines and the harassment of photographers. Nostalgic for New York, she left Los Angeles suddenly.

For several months she refused all offers of film roles. The studios accused her of acting in bad faith, and MGM decided to punish her by withholding her salary, while at home and under cover she was remaking the film of her life. During the winter of 1954, she learned she had been nominated for an Oscar for Best Actress in a Leading Role, in *The Country Girl*. Shortlisted with Judy Garland in the same category, for her part in *A Star is Born*, Grace thought she had no chance of winning. Nonetheless, several months later, in February 1955, she travelled to Hollywood for the ceremony.

She made a sensational entrance at the Oscars in a dress designed by her friend Edith Head. All eyes were on her. Grace Kelly was luminous. Seated in the hall next to her colleagues, she quietly waited along with everyone else for the crowning of Judy Garland. William Holden walked onto the stage, read out the names of the nominees, opened the envelope and announced with a radiant smile, 'The winner is Grace Kelly!' Amid thunderous applause, the cool blonde walked onto the stage at the peak of her career. After only five years as an actress, she had accomplished a considerable feat. Acknowledged by her peers, loved by the public, she had become the star of the moment.

After several days holidaying with her sister in Jamaica, she accepted an invitation to the Cannes Film Festival. She took herself off there for three days in April with the aim of promoting *The Country Girl* and attending a party arranged in her honour.

An unforgettable festival

The film festival opened on April 26, 1955 under the presidency of Marcel Pagnol. Arriving in Nice by train, Grace found the only French person she knew, her friend Jean-Pierre Aumont. Inseparable, they spent their days together. Their apparent friendship hid a complicit love affair. Looking to escape from the paparazzi, they took refuge at the Montana reserve in La Napoule, outside Cannes. Even so, Grace was pursued by photographers and journalists, and this lunch *à deux* resulted in a memorable photo of the couple. After a day spent in the countryside with MGM's man, she discovered on her return that everyone was already talking about her 'future marriage' to Jean-Pierre Aumont. Then Friday, May 6, 1955 arrived, the day that would change the course of her life for ever.

Caught up in a crazy timetable, that day Grace had to talk about her film to the press, give several interviews, go to the hairdresser, meet a prince in Monaco and attend a dinner organised in her honour. Behind schedule, she found Jean-Pierre Aumont while between two meetings and confided her wish to cancel her royal visit to Monaco. The rendezvous had been organised by *Paris-Match* and was in fact a photo session uniting for the first time the brightest Hollywood star and the most eligible man in Europe. Convinced by Jean-Pierre Aumont of the diplomatic importance of such a meeting, she agreed to go along with it. She chose a light dress decorated with flowers and left the hotel with her hair still wet.

Arriving on time, Grace, the journalist and the photographers entered the prince's palace. Rainier was late, detained at his villa at Beaulieu, but he had called ahead to say he would not be much longer. On his arrival, when she reverently greeted the prince, Grace regretted having put on that dress. Each intimidated by the other, the actress and His Highness set off for a walk around the gardens of the palace. After exchanging a few words the couple shook hands and politely said goodbye. Already, Rainier was smitten. He was to say that he had been charmed by her freshness, her maturity, her sensitivity and her culture. He could not detect any frivolity in her and he liked that about her. On her side, Grace said to her friends happily that he was 'charming'.

As the winners of the Cannes Festival were being announced, Grace had already left for Paris. She spent many happy days with Jean-Pierre Aumont. Hidden from the press in his La Malmaison home, she tasted the joys of a peaceful life, happy and surrounded by children, the actor's nephews. But Hollywood was calling and she had to return to play in *The Swan*.

Months later, Rainier finally confided in his chaplain, Father Tucker. He could not stop thinking about the vision – blonde as wheat and fresh-faced – that he could see by his side. As an American and keen to seal this union, the priest decided to do everything he could to reunite the prince and his muse. He wrote to Grace and confided in her the 'deep emotion' her memory evoked in the prince. She wrote back straight away that she hoped to meet him again on her next visit to Monaco ...

Satisfied by this response, without a moment's delay Father Tucker organised Prince Rainier's trip to the United States. He himself would accompany the prince. On board a transatlantic liner they crossed the ocean and arrived in New York several days before Christmas, 1955. Grace was still filming in Hollywood. Rainier and Father Tucker went to Philadelphia to stay with friends of the priest, the Austins. By happy coincidence, the Austins themselves had been invited to the home of ... the Kellys! And so Rainier found himself dining next to Grace, who had returned from California to spend Christmas with her family. Instantly adopted by the Kelly clan, Rainier III presented several trump cards: great sports enthusiast, fervent Catholic, ardent defender of family values, a prince adored by his people. After staying in Philadelphia for several days he went to New York to spend the New Year with Grace. It was there, only a week after they had got to know each other, that he proposed to her on New Year's Eve.

On their return to Philadelphia, Grace announced the news to her parents. Consistent as ever, the Kellys were... hesitant! It needed the intervention of Father Tucker to reassure them and to give them his word that Prince Rainier would make an excellent husband for their daughter. A few days later, on January 5, 1956, Grace and Rainier celebrated their engagement at a family dinner in Philadelphia. The people of Monaco heard the news and were exultant with joy. The first official photo of the couple was taken the next day at the Waldorf-Astoria in New York. The future princess had taken care not to wear high heels so as not to appear taller than her prestigious fiancé. She sent a telegram to Jean-Pierre Aumont to tell him of her engagement. Filming in Hollywood, the French comedian rejoiced in the happiness of the one they called the Philadelphia Princess. Like a lit fuse, the news blazed through the land. From the east coast of the United States to the south of Arizona, people talked about only one thing: would the star abandon her career or not?

In mid-January, Grace Kelly left to play in what would be her last film. Opposite Bing Crosby and Frank Sinatra, she sang for the first time on screen in *High Society*. The song, *True Love*, would be a gold record. Her only request during the film was to be allowed to wear her engagement ring. In March, she made an appearance at the Oscars, and the next day left Hollywood. Without knowing it, Grace Kelly had just turned a page in her life which would distance her for ever from the cinema studios.

On April 4, 1956, Grace set sail on board the liner *SS Constitution*, her destination Monaco. During the week-long crossing, she savoured her last moments as an ordinary woman. Torn between the heady anticipation of her life of splendour to come and the loss of all those she loved and who had made her, the future bride was anxious. Amid her parents and her friends on board ship, she tried to imagine what her life would be like without them from now on.

When the boat docked in Monaco, on April 12, it was cheered by a waiting crowd. Almost five thousand people had turned out to greet their princess. Church bells and ships' horns joined the cries of elation. Come to fetch her on board his yacht, Rainier III led his gift to his people through the crowd, and the couple left for the prince's palace as torrential rain started to fall that did not stop for several days.

It was such a fairy tale of modern times that the world's press could not resist reporting the details and behind-the-scenes preparations for what was already being called 'the marriage of the century'. Hour after hour, for a week, Grace Patricia Kelly was the most fêted woman in Europe. Leading up to the marriage ceremony, she lived the most 'diplomatic' six days of her life. From receptions to cocktail parties, from society *soirées* to balls, she did not have a single moment to savour the present. Her lovely smile was slowly replaced by a serious look. The closer her wedding day came, the more aware she became of how her future life would be.

Even though Grace and her parents stayed at the prince's palace, they did not see Rainier except at official ceremonies. Out of respect for convention, he stayed at his villa at Cap-Ferrat. Exhausted by the voyage and her social engagements, Grace lost almost five kilos in a few days. The whole world was preparing for the event, but the future princess seemed more remote than ever.

The marriage of the century

On Tuesday April 18, 1956, the civil ceremony took place. Within 15 minutes the prince and his wife had said 'Yes' and signed the register in the throne room of the palace. From now on they would be united by law. After a customary salute from the balcony of the palace, the couple invited the four thousand citizens of Monaco to an enormous garden party after the wedding. To a person, the Monegasques would not have missed this event for anything.

And finally the big day arrived, Wednesday April 19, 1956. Programmed down to the last minute, the day's organisation was equal to that of the Olympic Games. The schedule had no room for the slightest mistake or the briefest delay. At 11 a.m. the couple received the nuptial benediction in Monaco Cathedral under the watchful gaze of all the world's TV cameras and almost 30 million viewers.

Dressed in a tulle gown of silk and lace created by Helen Rose (an MGM costume designer), Grace, the future princess of Monaco, walked up the aisle. Among the guests were Ava Gardner, Marcel Pagnol, François Mitterand and Jean Cocteau. Alfred Hitchcock could not make the journey to admire the actress he fetishised in her last role. In view of the size of the event, SNCF and Air France had organised a 'bridge' between Paris and Monaco. Outside, there were almost 100,000 hushed people waiting to explode with joy. Time in the principality, as in most of Europe, seemed to have stopped.

The royal couple came out of the cathedral, to the resounding applause of the crowd. Shouts of joy mingled with boat horns and church bells. After a lunch attended by 600 guests, Her Serene Highness Princess Grace and Prince Rainier III of Monaco took their leave. At the end of the afternoon they drove to the port to rejoin the yacht *Deo Juvante II*.

The honeymoon stretched from Formentera (Ibiza) to Valencia, Palma, Jerez and the Bahamas and lasted almost two months. On the route home, anxiety seized the young woman at the thought of taking up her role as full-time princess. Her husband tried to reassure her as much as possible and told her more about the principality over which she would reign with him from now on. On her return, she threw herself body and soul into the mission she had set for herself: to become the perfect princess.

Despite her daily French lessons, she had real difficulty mastering the language. This unknown world, the obligations imposed by her position, the distance of her family and her homesickness did not take long to settle a melancholic expression on this beautiful face. Little by little, she felt she was losing her identity and was drowning in self-doubt. Feeling herself spied upon and criticised by the media, the aristocrats and the residents, she knew that the slightest mistake would be the source of intense discussion in a moment. In addition, the people were impatient to have a male heir, which seemed to be long in coming. They suspected her, they judged her. The Monegasques also frowned on her status as a film star. She once said, on this subject, 'The career of an actor is not well regarded in Monaco as it is in the United States.'

But Grace was a fighter. This was not her first battle and she increased her activities to put a stop to the rumours. She had the walls of the salons repainted and moved her own furniture and personal objects into the rooms. By degrees, the princess made her mark in her new life.

A mother before all

After having refurnished the State Room and various reception rooms in the palace, Grace appropriated a study for herself in the tower. Already, she felt the need to isolate herself from the view of the rest of the palace. After the interior spaces, the princess reworked a garden that she wanted to make varied and exotic. She kept a close eye on the landscaping, and not one plant, not one tree was put in place without her approval.

The lovely summer days were approaching and she discovered the Mediterranean warmth. By nature preferring more temperate climes, she suffered as much from the rising temperature as from the happy event that was announcing itself. Grace was expecting her first child. The Monegasques, mad with joy, prayed that it would be a little boy. A nursery was furnished near the parents' bedroom while the mother-to-be searched the shops for the necessary accessories. Five months' pregnant, she left in September 1956 for Philadelphia with Rainier. After having visited her parents, spending several days on holiday and meeting the American president, Eisenhower, the couple returned to Monte Carlo, where Grace lit up her first Christmas tree at the palace.

Her due date was now not far off, a room was equipped with all the medical equipment necessary, and several doctors and nurses were in place. To cover the event, several thousand journalists had descended on The Rock. On January 23, 1957, at 9.27, Her Serene Highness Princess Caroline Louise Marguerite of Monaco saw the light of day. At the age of 28, Grace had given birth to her first child. She would breastfeed her daughter as she would her other children.

Besotted with her newborn child, the princess would not let anyone enter the nursery and she herself saw to her child's needs. Barely recovered from her pregnancy, Grace fell pregnant again. This time the public held their breath … let it be a boy! If this were to be the case, it would be he who would inherit the throne. On March 14 1958, at 10.30 a.m. Albert Alexander Louis Pierre sounded his first cry. The royal couple and the Monegasques were ecstatic. The sovereign prince was born.

Several weeks after the birth of Albert, depression threatened once more. Grace therefore took on several projects. She furnished a projection room in the palace, and had a games room and a swimming pool installed. She also completely restored an old building bought by her husband. Situated more than 700 metres above sea level and a few minutes from Monaco, the property of Roc-Agel, which at first she had not cared for, would become her haven of peace. She controlled the metamorphosis of this place meticulously.

Surrounded by a vast landscape, it became the 'House of Happiness'. Every weekend the family took themselves down to what they would from now on call The Farm, where they lived alongside several cows, ponies, horses, parrots, hamsters, deer, chickens and other two- or four-legged creatures. In its huge, shaded space, the princess gave herself to her new passion: flowers. After having dried them she arranged them into collages and later into pictures. For his part, Prince Rainier occupied himself with the animals and announced proudly that he would make the butter for the house. The family spent happy hours here sheltered from the tumult of their life and the harassment of photographers.

Caroline, Albert and Stephanie

Applying herself to her role as mother with as much vigour as she had to her roles as actress and then princess, Grace instilled her values in her children. The temperaments of Caroline and Albert were radically opposite. Little Princess Caroline, joyful, bubbly, boisterous, cute and already independent, attracted attention at every moment. More reserved and timid, Albert (whom his mother affectionately called 'Albie') was a gentle child, affectionate and reflective. Despite his timidity, he was bright and playful. There was a balanced rapport at the heart of the family: Rainier was mad about his daughter whereas Grace adored her son. The Prince let his little *protégée* have anything her heart desired, whereas her mother never hesitated to restrain her. She tried to inculcate in Caroline notions of discipline, which the child tirelessly resisted. Devoted to his mother, Albert's admiration for her was without limit. Their relationship had something exclusive about it.

Encouraged by their mother, Caroline and Albert took part in sports from an early age. As their maternal grandmother said, 'One does less evil when one follows the rules of discipline of sport'. Grace had grown up with these values of order and physical performance. She educated her children to adopt this attitude towards life too. As a child, Albert played tennis, rowed, did judo, swam, took part in athletics and played football. Caroline rode horses, skied and swam. Because she herself was passionate about dance, Grace made lessons available at the palace. Stimulated and blossoming, Caroline and Albert had everything any child could dream of. A life-size carousel was even constructed for them within the walls of the palace.

The childrens' personalities affirmed themselves over the years. Involved in the ceremonial life of their parents, they learned very quickly how to behave in public. Even so, in a routine familiar to families across the world, Grace took her children to school, had lunch with them every day and let them choose the clothes she would wear.

During the summer of 1964, Her Serene Highness announced another pregnancy. Stephanie Marie Elisabeth was born on February 1, 1965. The smallest and last of the clan, the child was shielded from the media. Her parents did all they could to distance her from public duties. Also timid, Stephanie found comfort and protection in her big brother, Albert, whom she adored. They would play together for hours on end. As an adolescent, she wished above all to be a girl like any other. She was nicknamed 'the princess of jeans and sneakers'. Like her sister and brother, she took up dancing and sport.

Herself raised to be 'feminine', Princess Grace intended to transmit certain feminine skills to her daughters. Since their brother was destined to succeed their father to the throne, Caroline and Stephanie learned to sew and cook. By far the most rebellious, Caroline took a lot of persuading... The clash with her mother became apparent quite early. Grace first sent Caroline to a religious school, and at the age of 14 she went to St Mary's School, Ascot, in England. For two years she received a strict and austere education under the supervision of Sister Bridget. Affected by this separation, Prince Rainier phoned his daughter often.

After having spent her last school year in Paris with the Dames de Saint-Maur, Caroline achieved her *baccalauréat* in literature with honours. Grace and her two daughters installed themselves in their apartment on the Avenue Foch in Paris and returned to Monaco only on the weekends. Caroline, who was only 17 years old, was yearning for freedom from authority. She enrolled for a degree in political science and tasted the joys of outings with friends and to nightclubs. Determined to lead her life the way she wanted, the young woman quickly found herself written about in the press. Serious and independent at the same time, wishing for a normal life while enjoying the privileges of a princess, Caroline was in search of her identity. Beautiful and extravagant, she drew men to her. Grace watched this transformation, but felt helpless in the face of so much determination.

In 1976, Albert, who had stayed in Monaco, in turn obtained his *baccalauréat* and enlisted in the French navy. He completed seven months of military service on board the *Jeanne d'Arc*. On his return, he left for Amherst College in Massachusetts, in the United States. His mother suffered from this separation.

When Caroline was 18 she fell under the spell of a notorious playboy. Philippe Junot, 17 years older than her, initiated her into the jet set and night life of Paris. From spring 1976, their photos appeared in all the magazines. Outraged by this liaison, Grace and Rainier did all they could to make their daughter listen to reason, but in vain. Caroline married Philippe Junot on June 29, 1978. Dreaming of life as a couple and a family, Caroline quickly became aware of what made her different from her husband. To general relief, a divorce was granted in October 1980. Determined to erase this marriage completely, Grace went right to the Vatican to see it annulled.

Several months later, during the summer of 1981, the whole family went to the United States to witness Albert receiving his degree.

A busy woman

While overseeing the education of her children, Princess Grace gave the rest of her time to many charitable activities. Her husband designated her President of the Red Cross in Monaco in 1958, whereafter she tirelessly supported many different causes. From natural catastrophes abroad to aid for the elderly at home, refuges for young women, crêches, homes for children and Christmas for the poor, she battled poverty on all fronts. A devoted fundraiser and sensitive to human misery, she never said no to a request for help. In 1977, the United Nations recognised her work against world hunger.

She replied personally to the piles of letters sent to her from around the world. Every year she organised a ball to raise funds for the Red Cross, and also the Rose Ball, dedicated to the work of a selected charity. In 1965 she set up the Princess Grace Foundation to support promising artists at the start of their career, as well as medical research. Sought after by all sorts of organisations, she endlessly inaugurated ceremonies, balls and conferences. She lent her support to UNICEF and never missed the annual lighting of the Christmas tree at the palace and her distribution of gifts. As well as two presentations of awards for the Formula One Grand Prix, she also lent her unwavering support to the Academy of Classical Dance in Monaco. Passionate about plants, she created the Garden Club and presided over international flower-arranging competitions. An army of secretaries allowed Princess Grace to live life at top speed. But even though she was happy, the princess was not completely fulfilled. She concealed from the world a hole in her life... film. She, who from a young age had devoted all her energies to becoming an actress, suffered from being separated from the silver screen. Regularly offered roles by directors, she systematically refused any idea of filmmaking ... until 1962. That year, Alfred Hitchcock offered her the principal role in *Marnie*. Grace was overjoyed. With the approval of her husband, she announced her return to the cinema. The royal couple had planned to spend their holidays in the United States during the three months of shooting. But tied up with *The Birds*, the master of suspense was obliged to delay the shooting of *Marnie*. It was no matter – Grace was more motivated than ever.

It was then that the unthinkable happened. The news of the participation of the princess in a film was like a bomb going off in Monaco. Was it really appropriate for a princess to act in a film? Father Tucker went as far as saying: 'Grace, return to face the cameras? It's nonsense. Hollywood could not offer her a better role than the one she is playing now.' The Monegasques were ferociously against this project and even appealed to the Vatican to support their cause. Very disappointed, the princess gave in to popular opinion and declined Hitchcock's offer.

Following this episode, she was very sad and stayed locked in her room for several days. Eventually, as an alternative, she lent her voice in the years that followed, to commentating on documentaries on her life or on the principality, and she was increasingly in contact with the supporters of the seventh art. She went to Hollywood in 1967 to present an Oscar to Cary Grant and she never missed an homage to her friend Alfred Hitchcock. Her appointment to the board of Twentieth Century Fox in 1976 allowed her to go to the United States several times a year. In 1978, as if to thumb her nose at those who wanted to forbid the boards to her, she found a way of performing again. In the name of the World Wide Fund for Nature she set off on an American tour reading prose and poetry.

The last years

At the dawn of her fiftieth year, in 1979, Grace was still as luminous as ever, even though her inner flame was dimming. After years as the representative and devoted assistant of her husband, her children and the principality, she suffered terribly from loneliness. Her children, now adult, were spreading their wings. Alone in her golden palace, the princess did not have the heart for work. In addition, she had been weakened by successive colds and bronchitis and she felt tired. A fervent Catholic, she looked to her religion for comfort.

The accident

On Monday September 14, 1982, Grace got ready to leave Roc-Agel with Stephanie. She took the wheel of her Rover 3500. She was perfectly familiar with the mountain road and she knew the danger of the bends overhanging the gorge. Going around one of them she lost control of the car, which plunged down more than 40 metres. After rolling several times, the car hit a cement pillar and crashed into a private garden.

The princess and her daughter were both still alive when the car caught fire. A gardener armed with an extinguisher put out the flames and tried to pull them from the wreckage. Stephanie was first. But Grace was imprisoned by the crushed bodywork. Long minutes passed before the emergency services arrived. At the hospital in Monaco that carried her name, her condition was stated to be very serious. The injuries caused by the car's fall made the diagnosis very difficult. In a light coma, Grace was transported to a medical centre equipped with a scanner. Her condition grew worse, and at 22.30 Princess Grace was declared clinically dead.

The funeral was held a few days later, on Saturday September 18. Monaco's cathedral, draped in black, opened its doors to the guests and the family of the princess. Prince Rainier, overcome, was supported by Caroline and Albert. Stephanie was still in hospital and did not know that her mother had died. Diana Princess of Wales, Nancy Reagan, Danielle Mitterand, Frank Sinatra, Cary Grant and Jacky Stewart were among the 400 people present. In the afternoon, at 5 p.m. the family witnessed her entombment in the apse of the cathedral.

A new page in the history of Monaco had turned. The princess left behind three devastated children, a husband and a bereft public. The fairy tale that had enchanted the world had ended in tragedy. Real fairy tales exist only in the movies ...

«Fairy tales tell imaginary stories. I am a living person. I exist. The day someone tells of my life as a real woman you will discover the true person that I am.»

Princess Grace of Monaco

Grace Kelly's coat of arms which adorned all her personal effects from the moment of her marriage to Prince Rainier.

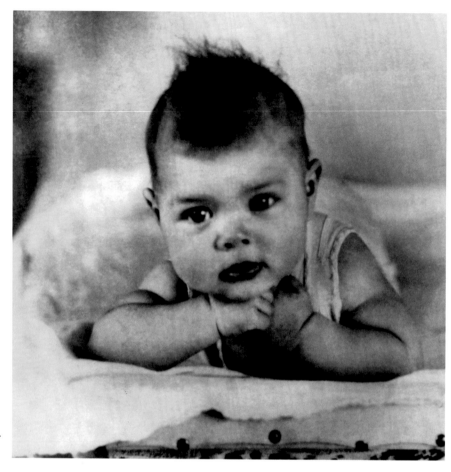

May 15 1930 Philadelphia, Pennsylvania: Grace Kelly at the age of six months.

1930 Philadelphia, Pennsylvania: Grace Kelly at the age of three months.

May 1931 Philadelphia, Pennsylvania: Grace Kelly aged one and a half.

1931 Philadelphia, Pennsylvania: Grace Kelly aged two, between her brother John Jack and her sister Peggy.

1937 Ocean City, New Jersey: Grace and her sister Margaret (Peggy) play on the beach.

1937 Ocean City, New Jersey: The Kelly family on holiday by the sea. From left to right: John, Margaret, Peggy, John Jr, Grace and Lizanne.

1938 Philadelphia, Pennsylvania: Grace Kelly at the age of nine, with her sister Lizanne.

1935 Philadelphia, Pennsylvania: Portrait of the family. In the first row, from left to right: Jack Kelly Jr (8), John B Kelly, Lizanne Kelly (2) and Margaret Kelly. Behind them, Grace (5) on the left and her sister Margaret (10) on the right.

November 11, 1936 New York, New York State: The Democrat senator, John B. Kelly, and his family on board the SS *Normandie*, en route to a short holiday in Europe. From left to right: Grace, Peggy, Mrs and Mr Kelly, John Jr., and in the front, Elizabeth-Anne, the youngest.

July 15, 1947 Henley, England: John Jr encouraged by his sisters Elizabeth-Anne and Grace before the start of the Henley Royal Regatta, which he would win.

1954 Ocean City, New Jersey: Grace Kelly spends the summer holidays with her family.

1954 Ocean City, New Jersey: Grace Kelly in front of the family's holiday home.

"For a TREAT instead of a TREATMENT — have an Old Gold"

Old Gold

1948 Hollywood, California: In October 1947, Grace was admitted to the prestigious American Academy of Dramatic Arts in New York. Determined to be financially independent, she worked after her classes as a model and posed for several advertising campaigns for shampoo, beauty creams and cigarette brands.

1948 Grace Kelly lent her support to a fundraiser for the participation of American athletes in the forthcoming Olympic Games.

NAME : Grace Kelly

VOICE : Improperly placed

TEMPERAMENT : Sensitive

SPONTANEITY : Youthful

DRAMATIC INSTINCT : Expressive

INTELLIGENCE : Good

GENERAL REMARKS : Good, full of potential

and freshness

1947 / Comments from the professors of the American Academy of Dramatic Arts, following Grace Kelly's audition. She was accepted and joined the academy in October 1947.

1954 / Portrait of Grace Kelly aged 24.

32

Preceding pages: June 9, 1949 Hollywood, California: The stars of the MGM studio to which Grace Kelly was under contract. From left to right, first row: Lionel Barrymore, June Allyson, Leon Ames, Fred Astaire, Edward Arnold, Lassie, Mary Astor, Ethel Barrymore, Spring Byington, James Craig, Arlene Dahl. Second row: Gloria DeHaven, Tom Drake, Jimmy Durante, Vera-Ellen, Errol Flynn, Clark Gable, Ava Gardner, Judy Garland, Betty Garrett, Edmund Gwenn, Kathryn Grayson, Van Heflin. Third row: Katharine Hepburn, John Hodiak, Claude Jarman, Jr, Van Johnson, Jennifer Jones, Louis Jourdan, Howard Keel, Gene Kelly, Christopher Kent (Alf Kjellin), Angela Lansbury, Mario Lanza, Janet Leigh. Fourth row: Peter Lawford, Jeanette MacDonald, Ann Miller, Ricardo Montalban, Jules Munshin, George Murphy, Reginald Owen, Walter Pidgeon, Jane Powell, Ginger Rogers, Frank Sinatra, Red Skelton. Fifth row: Alexis Smith, Ann Sothern, J Carroll Naish, Dean Stockwell, Lewis Stone, Clinton Sundberg, Robert Taylor, Audrey Totter, Spencer Tracy, Esther Williams, Keenan Wynn.

1954 Los Angeles, California: Esther Williams and Grace Kelly, in front of her home.

1950 Lizanne Kelly holds a mirror to help her sister Grace with her make-up.

November 17, 1952 Nairobi, Kenya: Grace Kelly and Clark Gable during the shoot of *Mogambo*, directed by John Ford.

1953 Nairobi, Kenya: Grace Kelly and Ava Gardner in *Mogambo* by John Ford.

1955 Cannes, France: Grace Kelly and Cary Grant in *To Catch a Thief*, by Alfred Hitchcock.

«I was never happy in Hollywood. There, everything is distorted by the importance people give to money.»

Grace

May 27, 1954
Hollywood, California:
Grace Kelly at her home
after a dip in her
swimming pool.

1956 Hollywood, California: Grace Kelly and Frank Sinatra on the set of the film *High Society*, by Charles Walters.

1955 New York: Grace Kelly during a photo session with the photographer Philippe Halsman.

1956 Hollywood, California: Grace Kelly on the set of the film *High Society*, by Charles Walters.

1955 New York: Grace Kelly at the Waldorf Astoria, during the party given to celebrate her engagement to Prince Rainier.

1956 Hollywood, California: Grace Kelly on the set of the film *High Society*, by Charles Walters.

«She never distanced herself from others. Even so, as soon as she came on set, everyone fell silent.»

Cary Grant

1956 Hollywood, California: Grace Kelly on the set of the film *High Society*, by Charles Walters.

December 2, 1977 Monaco: Princess Grace of Monaco attends a charity ball.

July 3, 1955 Philadelphia, Pennsylvania: During a charity event, Grace Kelly indulges in some candyfloss.

1956 Hollywood, California: Grace on the set of *High Society* by Charles Walters.

1954 New York: Portrait
commissioned for *Life*
magazine.

December 29, 1954
New York: Grace Kelly has just been elected among the most elegant women of the world in an annual survey held by an American institute of haute couture.

1954 Grace Kelly and Raymond Burr in *Rear Window*, by Alfred Hitchcock.

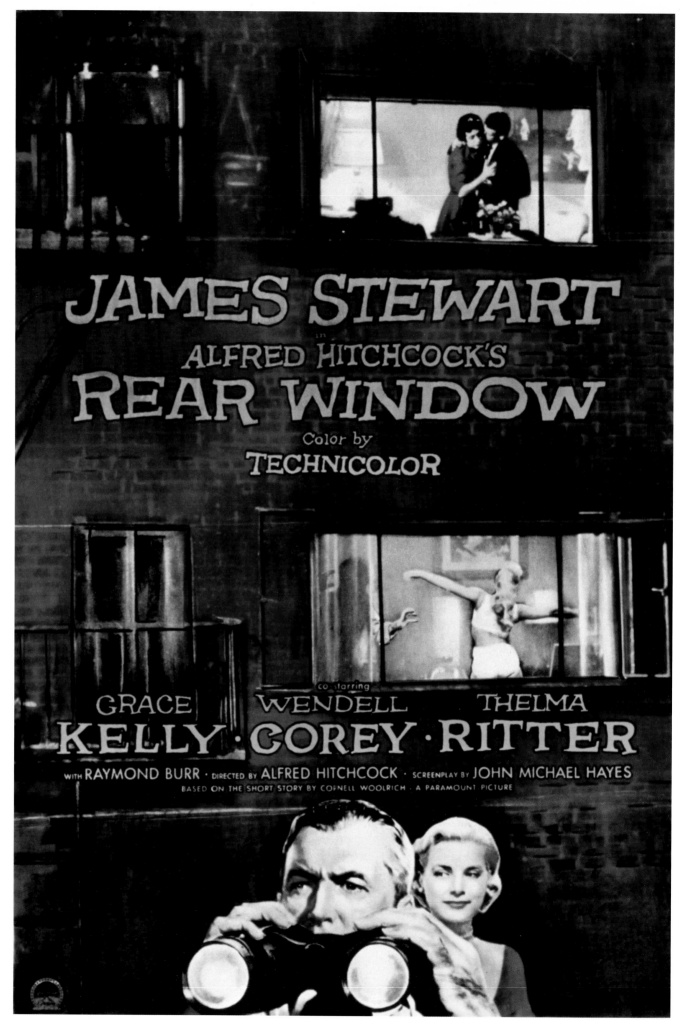

1954 Poster for the film *Rear Window*. It was the second film Grace Kelly did under the direction of Alfred Hitchock, after *Dial M for Murder*.

1954 James Stewart and Grace Kelly in *Rear Window*, by Alfred Hitchcock. The actress and the director would work again the following year in their third and last film together, *To Catch a Thief*. They would remain very close friends.

1955 Grace Kelly and Cary Grant in *To Catch a Thief*, by Alfred Hitchcock.

1955 Cannes, France: Grace Kelly and Cary Grant in *To Catch a Thief*, by Alfred Hitchcock.

1954 Los Angeles, California: Alfred Hitchcock, Grace Kelly and the fashion designer Oleg Cassini at the première of the film *Dial M for Murder*.

1954 In the La Victorine studios, Alfred Hitchcock directs Grace Kelly on the set of *To Catch a Thief*.

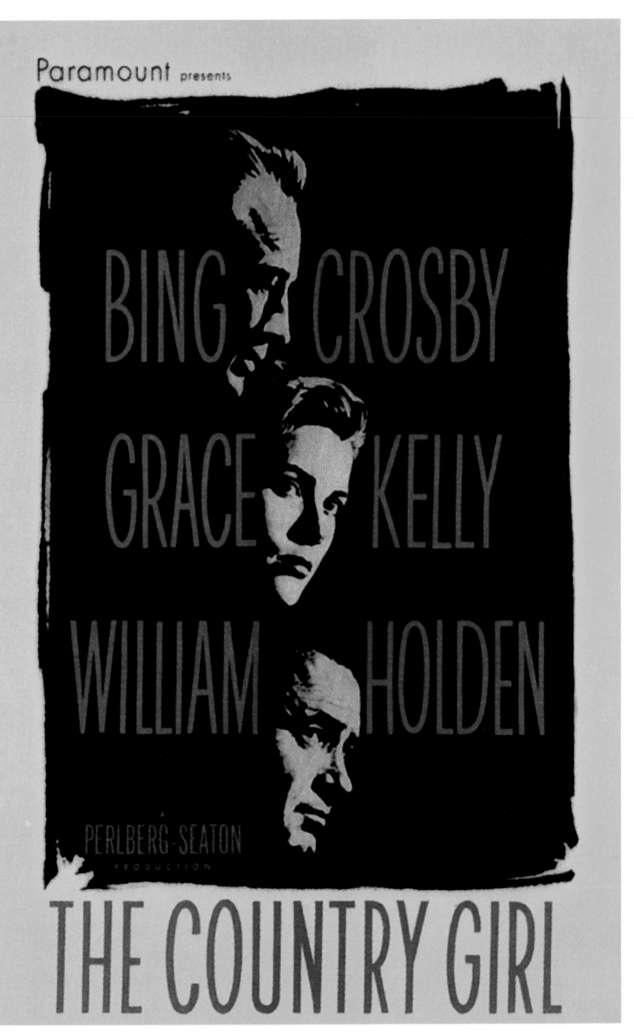

Paramount presents

BING CROSBY

GRACE KELLY

WILLIAM HOLDEN

A
PERLBERG·SEATON
PRODUCTION

THE COUNTRY GIRL

1955 Hollywood, California: Portrait of Grace Kelly taken during the filming of *The Country Girl*. She was 25 years old.

1955 Hollywood, California: Poster for the film *The Country Girl*, by George Seaton, with Bing Crosby, Grace Kelly and William Holden. Grace would receive the Oscar for Best Actress for her role in the film produced by Paramount.

«I came to success very quickly. Perhaps too quickly to value its importance.»

Grace

1955 Hollywood, California: Portrait of Grace Kelly at 25.

March 25, 1955 Hollywood, California: Grace Kelly on stage with Bob Hope after she had just received the Oscar for Best Actress for her role in the film *The Country Girl*, directed by George Seaton.

March 30, 1955 Los Angeles, California: Grace Kelly and Marlon Brando at the Oscars ceremony. Marlon Brando received the Oscar for Best Actor in a Leading Role for his part in *On the Waterfront*, by Elia Kazan, and Grace Kelly received an Oscar for Best Actress in a Leading Role for *The Country Girl*, by George Seaton.

«We fought, each of us in our own corner. That's what brought us closer together.»

Grace

Preceding pages : 1956 Hollywood. California: Fencing duel between Grace Kelly and Louis Jourdan in *The Swan*, directed by Charles Vidor..

74

May 6, 1955: Between a press conference and a gala dinner organised to promote her film, *The Country Girl*, at the Cannes Film Festival, Grace Kelly agreed to take part in a photo session. It was Gaston Bonheur, editor in chief of *Paris Match*, who conceived of this first meeting between the film star and Prince Rainier.

May, 1955 In the zoo that he had had installed at the foot of The Rock, the prince shows his wild animals to Grace Kelly, and in particular his latest acquisition, a Bengal tiger. Grace was impressed by the self-confidence of Prince Rainier, who did not hesitate to feed the animals by hand or to stroke them through the bars.

May 6, 1955 Monaco: Prince Rainier plays tour guide to Grace Kelly and shows her the panorama from the height of the palace ramparts.

1956 Hollywood, California: Grace
Kelly on the set of the film *The Swan*,
in which she performed with Alec
Guinness and Louis Jourdan.

March 25, 1956 New York: Grace Kelly goes riding in Central Park.

« I have always thought that a man who marries a famous woman loses some of his identity. I would not like to have a Mr Kelly. »

Grace

January 6, 1956 Philadelphia, Pennsylvania: Prince Rainier came to spend the end-of-year holidays in Philadelphia to get to know Grace's family and ask for her hand in marriage. He is seen here with Margaret and John Kelly, Grace's parents, on the day of the official announcement of the marriage to the press.

January 7, 1956 Philadelphia, Pennsylvania: The Kelly family and young Prince Rainier, shortly after announcing his future marriage. First row: Prince Rainier, Grace, Margaret and John B Kelly (Grace's parents), and Mrs Margaret Davis. Standing, from left to right: Mrs John B Kelly Jr, Donald C Levine (Grace's brother-in-law), John B Kelly Jr, George L. Davis (also Grace's brother-in-law), and Mrs Elizabeth-Anne Levine (Grace's sister).

Preceding pages: 1955 New York: Grace Kelly at the Waldorf Astoria, during the party held to celebrate her engagement to Rainier.

April 1956 Off the coast of Monaco: Grace Kelly surrounded by her parents and a group of friends, on board the liner SS *Constitution*, which they had taken from New York to the principality.

April 12, 1956 Azores: En route to Monaco and her marriage to Prince Rainier, Grace Kelly watches the sea while the ship SS *Constitution* anchors off the Azores.

April 19, 1956 Monaco: Press photographers on the alert to cover the marriage of Rainier and Grace. One thousand eight hundred journalists and photographers travelled to the principality to cover the event.

April 12, 1956 Monaco: Six days before her wedding, Grace Kelly arrived in Monaco on board Prince Rainier's yacht, the *Deo Juvante II*. She was welcomed by a jubilant crowd, 300 photographers and a shower of carnations, thrown from Aristotle Onassis's hydroplane.

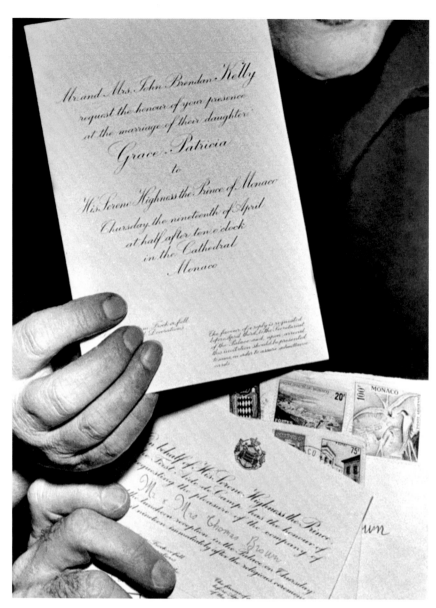

March 28, 1956 Pittsburgh, Pennsylvania: Invitation card for the royal wedding.

February 27, 1956 Monaco : Stamp issued by the principality on the occasion of the marriage of Rainier and Grace. Its face value was one franc.

April 19, 1956 Monaco: The wedding ceremony of the royal couple.

«Grace would have loved to run off and be married in a simple little chapel in the mountains. This unrealistic idea really enchanted me.»

His Serene Highness, Prince Rainier III

April 19, 1956 Monaco: Grace Kelly marries His Serene Highness Prince Rainier III.

April 19, 1956 Monaco: Grace Kelly marries His Serene Highness Prince Rainier III.

April 19, 1956 Monaco: The wedding procession leaves the cathedral. The couple would make their way around the town before returning to the palace.

Preceding pages : April 19, 1956 Monaco: The royal couple wave to their subjects after their marriage ceremony, a little before the garden party organised at the palace, to which all the Monegasques had been invited.

1956 Monaco: From the top of the staircase leading to the garden, the newly married royal couple wave to the guests.

1963 Monaco Palace: Portrait of Grace Kelly at the royal palace. She was then aged 33.

March 29, 1956 Monaco: View of the royal palace, illuminated for the marriage of Grace Kelly to Prince Rainier III of Monaco.

1963 Monaco Palace: Portrait of Grace Kelly.

Preceding pages: 1962 Monaco: Portrait of Grace Kelly, aged 32.

April 19, 1956 Monaco: The royal couple set off on their honeymoon on board the yacht *Deo Juvante II*, bought by the prince on the advice of his friend, the Greek tycoon Aristotle Onassis.

April 14, 1956 Monaco: Grace Kelly disembarks from *Deo Juvante II*, Prince Rainier's yacht, which he had sailed to fetch her from the SS *Constitution*, on her arrival from New York. To the sound of cannons the couple crossed Monaco by car, greeted by an enthusiastic crowd.

«Up to now, Grace has progressed with the ease of a trapezist. What I don't know is if the platform on which she has landed is not too narrow for her.»

Alfred Hitchcock

April 12, 1956 Monaco: Prince Rainier welcomes his future wife, Grace Kelly, on board his yacht after she disembarked from the SS *Constitution* on which she had sailed from New York. Almost 5000 people came to welcome her several hours later in the port of Monaco.

April 1958 Monaco: From the terrace of the palace, Princess Grace and Prince Rainier, who holds Caroline in his arms, present their son Albert, only a few days old, to their subjects.

March 19, 1958 Monaco: Princess Grace presents her son, Prince Albert Alexander Louis Pierre, aged five days. To the 140 titles Albert was blessed with on his birth, Rainier added that of Marquis of Baux.

1959 Monaco: Princess Grace and her two children.

1959 Monaco: Princess Grace and her son Albert, aged one year.

1954 Ajaccio, Corsica: Princess Grace of Monaco with her sister, Mrs Peggy Levine and her dog, Oliver.

July 22, 1967 Montreal, Canada: Princess Grace of Monaco smiles bravely on her departure from hospital after a miscarriage while the royal family were in Canada for the occasion of the Montreal World Expo in 1967.

1959 Monaco: Prince Rainier and Princess Grace spend a day sailing with their children Caroline and Albert, just off the shore of the principality.

«Princess Grace is in some way simultaneously my Minister of Youth, Recreation, Health and Solidarity.»

His Serene Highness Prince Rainier III

June 12, 1957 Princess Grace observes aerial operations from USS *Forrestal*, during manoeuvres in the Mediterranean. The royal couple spent a day at sea off the coast of Monaco.

March 23, 1961 Monaco: Princess Grace reads a story to her children, Albert and Caroline.

October 1962 Paris: On holiday, Princess Grace watches over her children, Caroline and Albert (left), on a swing in a public garden.

February 1962 Gstad, Switzerland: Princess Grace and her two children enjoying winter sports.

February 25, 1960 Gstad, Switzerland: Princess Grace holds Caroline, aged three, in her arms.

«My real difficulty was to become a normal person after having been an actress for so long. For me, at that time, a normal person was someone who made films.»

Grace

1960 Monaco: Princess Grace during the Monaco Grand Prix.

1962 Monaco: Princess Grace visits
the Bishop of Monaco.

January 8, 1961 Lourdes, France: Princess Grace on a pilgrimage.

April 27, 1965 Paris, France: Charles de Gaulle welcomes the royal couple on the balcony of the Elysée Palace.

May 24, 1961 Washington, DC : John F Kennedy receives the royal couple at the White House.

August 15, 1963 Nice, France: After a performance by the London Royal Ballet, Princess Grace of Monaco congratules the Russian dancer Rudolf Nureyev in the presence of the English actor, David Niven.

January 18, 1962 Monaco: Maria Callas with the Princess of Monaco, during the second International Festival of Television.

1963 Palma de Mallorca, Spain: The royal couple with the opera singer, Maria Callas.

«The publicity created around my brand image, made exemplary above others, sometimes annoyed me enormously. It's tiresome to be always cited as an example.»

Grace

Preceding pages: 1963 / Philadelphia, Pennsylvania: The royal couple at a reception.

136

February 1962 Gstad, Switzerland: Portrait of Princess Grace of Monaco, at 32 years old, taken during her holiday in the Alps.

1962 Monaco :
Princess Grace contemplates the
town from one of the palace terraces.

Monaco: The royal couple receive a visit from Karim Agha Khan.

«The only magic formula for bringing up children is to give them plenty of love.»

Grace

March 17, 1967 Montego Bay,
Jamaica: The royal family spends a
holiday in the sun. Princess Grace
relaxes beside the swimming pool
with her son Albert, aged nine.

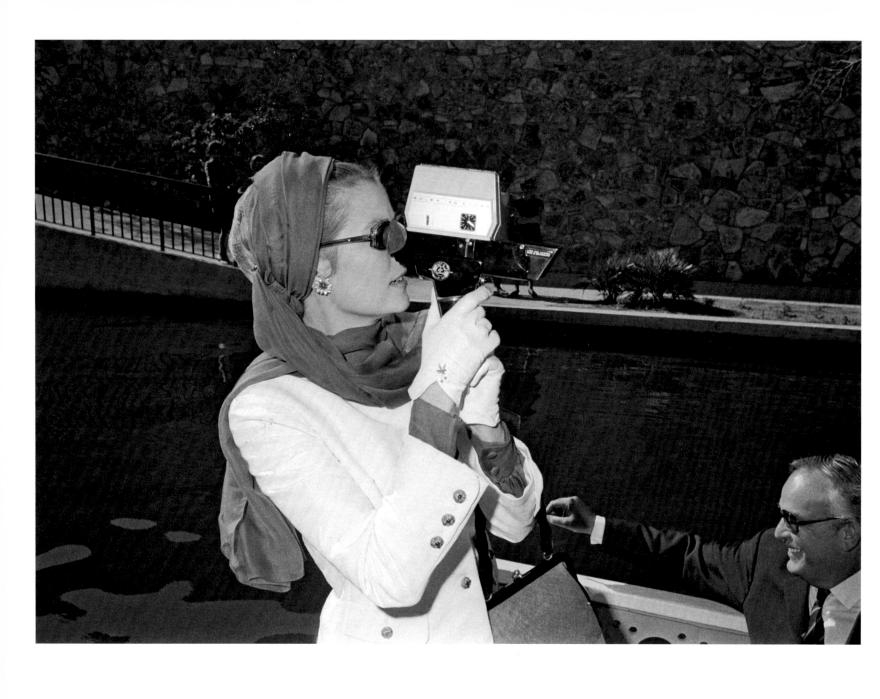

September 26, 1968 San Antonio, Texas: Grace Kelly and her husband at HemisFair 68, the world fair held in San Antonio, Texas.

May 17, 1965 Monaco: Prince
Rainier with his son Albert, aged 7.

«I am in favour of discipline. If you don't impose it on your children from an early age, life will impose it on them with a brutality of which no father or mother would ever be capable.»

Grace

1962 Monaco: Princess Grace visits an orphanage.

February 5, 1965 Monaco: Grace of Monaco poses with her daughter Stephanie, aged five days.

February 4, 1965 Monaco : Prince
Albert and Princess Caroline are
introduced to their new little sister,
Princess Stephanie, four days old.

147

June 3, 1966 Prince Rainier and Princess Grace spend a few days on a holiday cruise, on the liner *Renaissance*.

March 1966 Monaco: Prince Rainier, Princess Grace and their son Albert go sailing, off the coast of the principality.

April 19, 1963 Seville, Spain: The royal couple attends a flamenco festival. The princess is wearing a traditional Andalusian costume. Later in the evening, Grace and Albert would be joined by John F Kennedy and his wife, Jackie

«Good manners are becoming more and more rare. Protocol is a very effective barrier against all sorts of attacks.»

Grace

Preceding pages: May 5, 1956 Palma de Mallorca, Spain: During their honeymoon trip, Grace of Monaco and Prince Rainier stopped in Spain and attended a corrida. The matador Bernardo dedicates his first bull to the princess.

156

August 10, 1968 Monaco: Princess
Grace of Monaco at the Red Cross
Gala.

157

July 5, 1967 London, England: The royal couple on their way to visit Montreal Expo 67 arrive at Victoria Station. Prince Rainier holds his daughter Stephanie , aged two and a half, in his arms. Pregnant with her fourth child, Princess Grace made use of the London stop to meet potential child-minders. Unfortunately, she miscarried three weeks later..

September 15, 1966 Ocean City, New Jersey: Princess Grace of Monaco spends two weeks' holiday with her family in her native land, in her parents' seaside holiday home. She is with her children, Caroline, aged nine, Albert, eight, and Stephanie, one and a half years old.

November 20, 1958 Monaco: Prince Rainier and Princess Grace leaving a religious ceremony on Monaco's National Day.

November 21, 1968 London, England: Princess Grace of Monaco and Prince Rainier take part in a motor race in London, with their children Caroline, Stephanie and Albert.

March 1966 Monaco: Prince Rainier watches his children Caroline, Albert and Stephanie having fun on the carousel which he had had installed for them in the palace gardens.

March 1966 Monaco: Caroline takes her little sister Stephanie for a drive in her 'roadster'.

November 22, 1963 Monaco: During a visit to Luna Park, Princess Grace tries her hand at target shooting, under the amused eye of Princess Caroline, to whom her mother had just given a ball.

November 22, 1963
Monaco: Princess Grace has fun with her children at Luna Park. To her right are Princess Caroline and Prince Albert.

165

«There are many little ways to enlarge your child's world. Love of books is the best of all.»

Grace

1968 Monaco: Photo of the family in the palace gardens. From left to right: Caroline, Princess Grace, Stephanie, Albert and Prince Rainier.

September 15, 1967 Venice, Italy: Princess Grace of Monaco makes her entrance at a masked ball organised at the Rezzonico Palace. The guests had all arrived at this very popular charity event in gondolas, along the Grand Canal.

March 15, 1969 New York: Sophia Loren and Princess Grace of Monaco take part in a gala dinner on the occasion of the inauguration of the Hall of the Americas.

April 10, 1977 St Jean Cap Ferrat, France: Princess Grace of Monaco attends the show of Nina Ricci's Spring-Summer Collection, held at the Villa Ephrussi de Rothschild.

1968 Monaco : Princess Grace goes shopping in the principality.

July 28, 1972 Monaco: Caroline, aged 15, has just returned from her school in England and is rediscovering the Beach Club pool. Her mother Grace is attending a swimming competition.

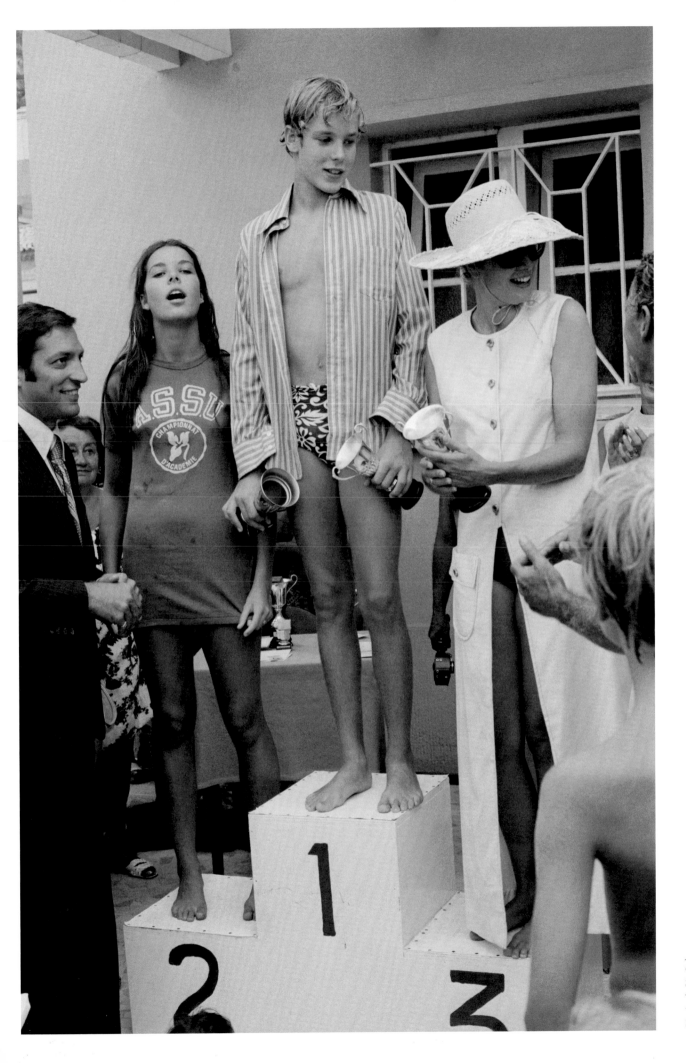

August 26, 1971 Monaco: Princess Grace holds the cup of her daughter Stephanie, who shared the podium with Albert and Caroline, all three of them team winners in a Family Swimming Relay competition.

173

Preceding pages: March 30, 1977 New York: In the port of New York, Grace of Monaco christens the new liner *Cunard Princess*, whose route would link New York and Bermuda.
June 10, 1971 Philadelphia, Pennsylvania: Princess Grace arrives at Philadelphia airport, in the land of her childhood, where she will visit her parents.

September 20, 1971 Monaco: Princess Grace accompanies her daughter Stephanie on her first day at school, while Albert, aged 12 years, will go on to his high school.

« You were the queen of the screen. You have become the most beautiful of princesses. »

John Fitzgerald Kennedy

April 29, 1974 New York:
Princess Grace and her brother Jack
leaving the presentation of a film in
memory of Alfred Hitchcock.

August 9, 1974 Monaco: Young Prince Albert attends his first Red Cross Ball, accompanied by Princess Grace, Prince Rainier and Princess Caroline.

London, England: At Heathrow airport, Princess Grace and her daughter Stephanie and Caroline leave for their Easter holidays in the United States. Grace had made a detour to London to catch up with her son who was studying there.

« The freedom of the press is such that it deprives individuals of their own. »

Grace

August 2, 1976
Philadelphia, Pennsylvania:
During the 41st International
Eucharistic Congress,
Princess Grace of Monaco
makes a short speech at
a session dedicated to
family life.

1964 Princess Grace poses for an artist.

1964 Princess Grace between the artist and her canvas.

«I would like people to remember me as a very humane person, sympathetic to the troubles of others.»

Grace

Preceding pages: February 25, 1978 Pittsburgh, Pennsylvania: For the first time in 26 years, Grace of Monaco performed on a stage in the United States. She had agreed to take part in a reading of poems by D H Lawrence, in the company of Richard Pasco.

1972 Portrait of Princess Grace of Monaco taken at the palace.

December 12, 1982 Paris, France: Princess Stephanie, Prince Albert, Princess Caroline and Prince Rainier III.

1971 Tehran, Iran: Princess Grace attends the celebrations of the 2,500th anniversary of the birth of the Persian Empire, organised by the Shah of Iran in the Aryamehr Stadium, now called the Azadi Stadium.

September 14, 1982

Monaco - Death of Princess Grace

Preceding pages: October 1977 Paris, France: Princess Grace of Monaco on the roof of the Garnier Opera, after she had appeared in a documentary about the legendary Kirov Ballet School in Leningrad.

September 15, 1982 Monaco: After the announcement of the death of Princess Grace, the royal guards wear a black armband as a sign of mourning..

September 15, 1982 Monaco: Grace Kelly died on September 14, 1982 at 22.15. The next morning, more than 4,000 newspapers around the world would headline the sad news.

September 17, 1982 Monaco : Throughout the principality, flags flew at half mast.

September 18, 1982 Monaco: The funeral of Grace of Monaco. At 10.30 the coffin, covered by a white flag bearing the arms of the House of Grimaldi, left the palace and was taken slowly towards the cathedral, carried by 12 members of the Brotherhood of the Black Penitents. Behind the coffin, Prince Rainier is supported by his daughter Caroline and son Albert and followed by Grace's two sisters and brother.

September 1982 Monaco: From 8 am a large crowd started to gather in front of the cathedral to pay their last respects to the princess.

September 18, 1982 Monaco: The funeral of Grace of Monaco. The princess's coffin was placed at the entrance to the cathedral, while a sea of royalty, heads of state and film stars flowed round it into the cathedral.

September 18, 1982 Monaco: Prince Rainier leaves the cathedral, with his son Albert and daughter Caroline, after the funeral Mass. Princess Stephanie, although recovering, was still under observation in hospital, following the car accident.

September 18, 1982 Monaco: The funeral of Princess Grace of Monaco.

September 18, 1982 Monaco: After the funeral, Prince Rainier and his children leave the cathedral to return to the palace.

«Grace, beautiful and elegant, brought a touch of magic to the court. She used her name to promote the image of Monaco across the world.»

Nadia Lacoste - Secretary to Princess Grace of Monaco

1990 Monaco: Albert, heir apparent, aged 32 years, poses in front of a portrait of his mother, Grace, in the royal palace.

Acknowledgements

Pierre-Henri Verlhac would like to thank Catherine Alestchenkoff, Jean-Luc Allavena, Hervé Irien, Jean Mirat and Claude Palmero for their support during this project.

I dedicate this book to my extraordinary mother. To all our future giggles...
Yann-Brice Dherbier

The authors wish to thank His Serene Highness Prince Albert II for having made this venture possible and Tommy Hilfiger, for supplying this book with the foreword it deserves. Also Ginta Gelvan, Michele Giacalone, Sanne Krom, Quohnos Mitchell and Reine Willing for their enthusiasm and energy in ensuring this photographic work reaches as many people as possible. Renaud Sauteret for the layout design for this seventh volume of the collection 'A Life in Pictures'.

And also:
Xavier Barral, Pascal Beno, Marie-Christine Biebuyck, Eva Bodinet, Elisabeth Eulry, Claudine Legros, Barbara Mazza, Patrick Olier, Jessica Plobete, Michèle Riesenmey, Catherine Seignouret, Michael Shulman, Steve Spelman and Catherine Terk.

Further Reading

Chère Princesse Grace / by Jacqueline Monsigny / Michel Lafon, 2002
Grace / by Bertrand Meyer-Stabley / Pygmalion, 1999
Grace Kelly / by Philippe Barbier & Jacques Moreau / PAC, 1986
Grace of Monaco, an Interpretive Biography / by Steven Englund / Doubleday, 1984
Grace / by Robert Lacey / A Contrario, 1984
Grace, the story of a Princess / by Phyllida Hart-Davis / St Martin Press, 1982
The History of Monaco / by J-B Robert / P.U.F., 1973
Prince Rainier of Monaco / by Peter Hawkins / William Kimber, 1966

Picture Credits